M. J. GROVER

Agate Hunting on the Oregon Coast

A Guide to the 40 Best Agate Hunting Sites

All effort has been made to provide accurate information in this book. The author assumes no liability for accidents or injuries sustained by readers engaging in activities described here. All persons are advised that changes (man-made or natural) can occur at any time that may create hazardous conditions. Laws can change at any time, and it is each individuals responsibility to be up to date with the latest regulations.

Whilst we endeavor to keep this information up to date and accurate, any reliance you place on this material is done strictly at your own risk.

For more rockhounding adventures go to agatehunting.com

First edition

ISBN: 978-1-7362750-0-9

This book was professionally typeset on Reedsy.
Find out more at reedsy.com

Contents

Introduction

The more I travel, the more certain I am that the Oregon Coast is one of the most beautiful and magical places on Earth.

Having spend countless days at the coast over the past 20+ years, I never get tired exploring every nook and cranny that it has to offer.

And there is certainly no shortage of places to explore! The Pacific coastline stretches for 363 miles, and every square inch of it is open to the public. A landmark piece of legislation in 1967 known as the *Beach Bill* established public assess and right of ways to the entire Oregon Coast.

In addition to dozens of state parks that span the length of the state, there are literally hundreds more places that you can access the Pacific Coast. From any coastal town or roadside turnout along Highway 101, you can simply "head west" and you shouldn't have much trouble finding access to the beach.

So if you are on the hunt for agates, you've got plenty of places to look. And here we get to the reason that I decided to write this guide book.

Yes, we have access to 363 miles of the Oregon Coast, but exactly where are the best places to find agates? All beaches are NOT created equal for agate hunting.

On my many trips to the Oregon Coast over the years I started finding some beautiful agates, jaspers, and other beachcombing treasures. I was hooked. I loved the treasure hunt. **But many unproductive trips taught me that certain areas were much, much better than others.**

If you don't know where to go, there's a good chance you will go home empty-handed.

I started researching different areas and trying to figure out where to spend my time for the best results. There was certainly information out there, but it was scattered and vague. I was surprised that there weren't really any good guide books available. The rockhounding books that were available only mentioned a small selection of well-known areas that overlooked some of the better beaches.

I hope this guide book helps to fill that void. **Out of hundreds of miles of coastline and hundreds of different accesses points along the Oregon Coast, I have selected 40 of the very best beaches for agate hunting.** It's surely not all of them... and I have no doubt that there are still a few "secret" beaches out there for you to find. Use this as a guide and don't be afraid to explore some new spots too!

This list was compiled with many years of on-the-ground research and personal exploration. I have visited each of these sites several times, and every picture in this book was take by me.

I hope this book helps you find some amazing agates.

Happy hunting!

What are Agates?

Agate is a form of chalcedony that is usually semitransparent to translucent. If you find a rock on the beach that you can see through (even if it's foggy) then it's probably an agate. If a rock completely blocks light from passing through it, then it is not an agate.

Agates found on the Oregon Coast were formed in an area that had intense volcanic activity. This volcanic activity produced silica. Once the eruptions were over in a given place and the rain fell on the volcanic ashes, the silica in the ashes dissolved in the rainwater.

As the silica concentration in the water became high the water turned into a silica gel which was held in cavities or "vugs" in the lava and slowly crystallized into microcrystalline quartz. Erosion takes places and this material eventually finds its way into the ocean.

If the water-silica solution that crystallized to form the agate had impurities in it then various colors are the result, and these impurities are what make agates so beautiful.

Agates are often comprised of banded materials which can be identified by closely observing a specimen using a loupe or microscope. Hold the stone up to a flashlight and see if the light glows through it.

Select pieces that show nice banding are some of the most attractive agates that you can find. As you learn to find agates, you will soon realize that there are average agates, and then there are real "trophy" agates. No two pieces are exactly alike.

Most of the agates you can expect to find will range in size of a jellybean on up to the size of a walnut. Put in enough time and you might get lucky and find one much larger than that. There are big ones out there!

Agates come in a wide array of colors, but certain colors will be more abundant depending on the area that you search. Along the beaches of the Pacific Ocean you will most commonly find agates ranging from clear, yellow to orange. There are even dark agates that are deep blue, purple and nearly black.

Regulations: Collecting Agates on the Oregon Coast

Collection of small quantities of various beach materials is perfectly legal according to Oregon law. This includes things like agates and other rocks, driftwood, seashells and other non-living things that you might find while walking along the sea shore.

Not only is it legal, most towns along the coast actively encourage beach-combers to come and explore their beaches. Events like the popular Finders Keepers program that distributes glass floats in Lincoln City and the Yachats Agate Festival are reminders that rockhounds and beachcombers contribute to the local economy.

Of particular importance are the restrictions on personal use and defined quantities. There are a few different laws (ORS 390.705, ORS 390.725, OAR 736-021-0090) regarding collections of beach rocks and marine materials. Most of them do not apply to casual beachcombers, but below are a few important highlights quoted directly from Oregon law:

(4) A person may remove small quantities of natural products from the ocean shore state recreation area for personal use without a permit as provided in subsections (a) and (b). However, the department may restrict removal of natural products to specific areas of the ocean shore state recreation area, by quantities of material,

and by time of year.

(a) Souvenirs that may serve as a reminder of a person's ocean shore visit and may include a small quantity of agates and other rocks, driftwood, and similar non-living items collected for non-commercial, personal use in accordance with ORS 390.705 and 390.725. For items such as agates, sand and cobble, each person collecting must use an individual container and may not combine collections in the same container with another person. Unless otherwise restricted by the department, a person may remove:

(A) Agates and other non-living items such as shells, stones, and fossils loose on the ground, in small quantities, defined as no more than a one-gallon volume container per person per day; up to three gallons per person per calendar year.

(B) Sand: no more than a five-gallon volume container per person per day; up to 20 gallons per person per calendar year.

(C) Cobble: no more than a five-gallon volume container per person per day; up to 10 gallons per person per calendar year.

(D) Driftwood, for non-commercial purposes, as follows:

(i) No more than one cubic yard (3 ft X 3 ft X 3 ft) per person per day; up to three cords per person per calendar year.

(ii) Driftwood removal is restricted to wood that can be loaded by hand only. A person may not use mechanized loading or removal equipment. The department must approve chainsaw use.

So basically, as long as you are collecting reasonable quantities of agates, jaspers, driftwood, invertabrate fossils, etc. and it is for personal use only then you are just fine. Enjoy the hunt!

Collecting Tools & Gear

One great thing about looking for agates is that it takes no special equipment. Anyone can take a walk on the beach and find all the agates their heart desires without spending a dime on special supplies.

With that said, there are a few things that can make your agate hunting trip easier and certainly more comfortable.

One handy tool that I see a lot of people using is a sand dipper. This is a long handled tool that looks like a golf club with a small scoop at the bottom. You can use it to scoop up rocks without bending over.

If you find it difficult to bend down then this can really make beachcombing a lot more pleasant. You can buy them relatively inexpensively, but I've also seen homemade ones that people made using a broom handle and bent spoon.

The other types of special gear that I would recommend is comfortable clothing, boots and rain gear. No matter what time of year you are visiting, there is ALWAYS a chance of getting rained on at the Oregon Coast. In the fall, winter and spring you can pretty much bet on it. Many of the best days I've ever had agate hunting on the coast were in the cold, wind and rain.

Come prepared so you can enjoy your adventure.

Other Beachcombing Treasures

This book is about agate hunting, but of course there are many other fun things to find when you are exploring Oregon's beaches.

Jasper

For me, a nice jasper is as big of a treasure as an agate. Jaspers are structurally very similar to agates. They are both chalcedony, a microcrystalline quartz. However, while agates are transparent or translucent, jaspers are opaque. Light will not pass through them and they don't have the same "glassy" appearance that agates have.

Jaspers are still very beautiful though. They come in a wide variety of different colors. This variation in color will depend on the impurities within each stone. It is actually the impurities that give each piece of jasper their unique color. They are found in yellows, greens, orange, reds, purples, and other neat color variations.

You may also find a jasper that appears to have small pockets within the stone that appear to be more transparent. These are actually a mix of both jasper and agate, and are often referred to as "jasp-agates." Some of these can be very beautiful too, and will make a nice addition to your collection.

Fossils

Throughout this book we will mention some beaches that are also great for fossil hunting. Most of the fossils found along the Oregon Coast are marine invertebrates. Dozens of different species have been found and identified.

The sources of these fossils are ancient sea beds that have eroded over millions of years, releasing fossil specimens that are eventually washed up on the shore. The cliffs along much of the coastline from Lincoln City down to Newport are lined with ancient sedimentary sandstones and siltstone dating back roughly 15 million years. These cliffs contain many fossils that erode and continuously source new fossils.

It is worth mentioning that collecting of invertebrate fossils (critters without backbones, most commonly clams and snails) is legal, but they cannot be sold commercially without a permit. Shell fragments are common. Complete specimens are less common but you can still find them if you spend enough time looking.

You are not allowed to collect vertebrate fossils (bones) without a permit. They are not as common, but on rare occasions things like complete jaw bones, teeth and vertebrae from whales, sharks and sea lions are found. These cannot be legally collected, and if you think you have found one it should be reported to the Hatfield Marine Science Center in Newport.

Petrified Wood

There are many different kinds of petrified wood to be found along the coast. Teredo wood is one of the most popular. It will usually appear as rounded brown or black rocks that have holes in them resembling Swiss cheese. These holes are actually tunnels that were bored into wood by the Teredo Clam while in its larval form. Teredo wood is generally easy to spot because of its unique texture.

Other petrified wood from various species can be found. Look for the tell-tale sign of growth rings and parallel lines to separate petrified wood from other beach stones.

Driftwood

I'm sure it's no surprise that the Oregon Coast has abundant driftwood. Pieces with fun, intricate shapes can be found just about anywhere, though hunting is always best after a good storm. They make great decorations around the home, and can be used for a variety of art projects.

Glass Fishing Floats

Fishing floats are one of the rarest and most treasured finds for Oregon beachcombers. While they have been used by various cultures around the world, the ones that wash up on the Pacific coastline come from Asia. They are round glass balls that were used to float fishing nets.

These floats were produced by the hundreds of thousands in the early 1900s, primarily in Japan. They were made in a variety of colors and sizes. Of course, fishermen would lose their fishing gear from time to time, and the floats would be lost, making their way across the Pacific Ocean before eventually ending up somewhere along the coastline.

Thought the 19th century, Japanese fishing floats were common along the

Oregon Coast. They are rare now, but occasionally show up even today. Major weather events that produce strong west winds bring them to shore.

Modern Glass Art Floats

Japanese floats are pretty rare these days, but hunting for modern glass floats is more popular than ever.

Every year, glass artists in Lincoln City scatter roughly 3,000 fancy glass floats on the beaches for visitors to find anywhere from Road's End (just north of Lincoln City) down to Siletz Bay. The "Finders Keepers" program is a fun idea to encourage tourism to the area that has been going on since the mid-90's.

The town of Gold Beach also hides some glass floats from February through April. You can bring tagged floats to the visitor center in town and maybe win a prize. They are hidden between the Rogue River jetty down to Kissing Rock. They are hidden above the high tide amongst the grass and driftwood.

Seashells

Oregon isn't particularly well-known for its seashells. While we certainly don't have the abundance or variety of shells that warmer climates have, you can still find some nice shells from time to time.

Perhaps the most common prize is the sand dollar. They are flat and white with a "star" on the top. These are fairly common is certain areas under the right conditions. They are usually broken, but you can find them intact if you hunt hard enough. Remember, keep out of areas designated as Marine Gardens, as collecting is strictly off-limits there.

Sea Glass

Sea glass is simply a shard of broken glass that has spent years tumbling in the ocean. The result is a tiny, frosty "pebble" of glass. Clear, green and brown are going to be the most common, but you can get lucky and find blues, reds and purples. For some, these are the ultimate beach treasure.

Gold

Most people are quite surprised to hear that they can find gold at the Oregon Coast. Actually, there was a short-lived gold rush to the beaches of southern Oregon during the 1860s, and mining continued on and off for many years.

The gold is found as tiny particles within the beach sands. You can use a standard gold pan to carefully separate those tiny flakes of gold from lighter sand.

The best beaches are in Southern Oregon. Gold Beach, Whiskey Run, Cape Blanco, and Port Orford are all places that are known to have gold. You may need to do a bit of "prospecting," but the best spots are generally easy to find because you will see black sands. These are sands that contain iron, and are heavier than the lighter colored sands. These black sands are where you will find the gold.

Don't expect to get rich, but it's pretty fun to do, and yet another treasure that you can find on the Oregon coast.

Safety on the Coast

I don't want to exaggerate the risks associated with agate hunting, but at the same time it is worth mentioning them so that we all have a safe trip while exploring the beaches of the Oregon Coast. Agates certainly aren't so important that we should risk our health and safety.

Of course millions of people visit the Oregon Coast every year without incident. Unfortunately, every year sees a few people who die from weather and waves. So lets take a quick look at some dangers so we can make sure that we are reasonably prepared.

Weather

Everyone knows that rain is a part of life in this part of the world. Be prepared to get wet. Even on a warm, sunny day, rainclouds can blow in quickly and change drastically. Winters along the coast are generally predictable... wet and cold.

Be prepared with the proper gear and clothing before you head out. Dress in several layers and always have some good rain gear with you, so you are ready for whatever comes. Wear a good pair of boots during the the winter months and keep them oiled up!

Storms & Waves

Agate hunting and winter storms go hand-in-hand as far as I am concerned. Those nasty storms that blow over the Pacific Ocean and pummel the Pacific Northwest with wind and rain also strip sand off the beaches and expose agates and jaspers. Serious agate hunters love a good storm.

However, these storms create epic waves that must be respected. Never turn your back on the mighty Pacific Ocean. Large waves can come at you unexpectedly and ruin a good day. You may think this sounds like an exaggeration, but people die every year on the Oregon Coast because of these "sneaker waves."

This may be less of a concern if you are on a long sandy beach, but often we agate hunters find ourselves scrambling around in rocks, exploring low tide pools, and amongst driftwood and other structures. Large waves can easily cause a person to lose their footing, slip down among large rocks, or get trapped under driftwood. Huge pieces of driftwood can be moved by just a few inches of water, so never stand or sit on driftwood near the waves.

Wild Animals

Wildlife is one of the things that makes the beaches so fun to visit. While most of them aren't all that dangerous, we still need to be respectful of the critters out here.

Seals and sea lions are common along the Oregon Coast. You need to keep your distance from them. During calving season in particular it is imperative that you keep your distance. Make sure your kids are aware, and keep dogs leashed during this time of the year. Not only is it the safe thing to do, but it's also illegal to harass wildlife.

There are bears and mountain lions in the Coast Range. You aren't very likely to encounter them if you are walking on the beach, but you might if you explore some of the creeks and rivers that drain into the Pacific Ocean. The best advice if you encounter a bear or mountain lion is to give them their space, and slowly back away. Actual attacks on humans are exceedingly rare and nothing to be overly concerned about in my opinion.

Plants & Bugs

A more real concern you might encounter are bugs! There are all kinds of flying, stinging critters that you might encounter. Ticks are not uncommon during the spring and summer. Definitely bring some insect repellant with you, particularly during the warmer months.

There are a few plants to avoid. Most noteworthy is Poison Oak, which can really ruin your day if you get into it. You'll probably be fine if you are simply beachcombing, but it does grow in the mountains nearby. Blackberries and other thorny plants are also abundant.

Cliffy Areas

Use caution when exploring around rocky areas and along cliff walls. The ocean waves erode and undercut them and can cause sand, dirt and rocks to fall on your head. Rocks can be slippery and a large wave can easily knock a person down if you are standing on one. Use caution.

Exploring the Beach

Don't let any of this scare you away from visiting the beach. Every year millions of people have a safe and fun trip that goes by without incident, so there is no need to be fearful. I simply want people to be prepared, just as with any outdoor adventure that you might have.

All in all, searching for agate is a safe and fun activity perfect for anyone. Just be smart and don't forget the rain gear!

When is the Best Time to Go Agate Hunting?

This book tells you *WHERE* to go, but much of the time it is just as important to know *WHEN* to go. Timing is everything when you are agate hunting.

Even the very best beach on the coast might not produce a single agate if conditions aren't right. Once you've found a good beach, there's just one more thing you need... **GRAVEL!** Productive beaches will have exposed gravel beds, or at least a nice assortment of rocks scattered about. This is where you will find agates and jaspers. If the beach you are visiting is solid sand and completely devoid of gravel, your odds of success will be low.

Best Season

Prime agate hunting season runs from November through April. This is when big storms wash up fresh agates and jaspers, and strip away the accumulated sands that cover up the agate beds.

Yet the height of tourist season on the coast runs from May through September. **Therefore, the time of year that most people are here to visit is the worst time of year to be looking for agates.** The agates are still there, but you can't see them because they are covered by inches or feet of sand.

Does that mean that you won't be able to find an agate during the summer? Certainly not. You can absolutely find agates throughout the year, but winter is when you can expect to find them consistently.

This makes it even more important to know where the best agate hunting beaches are. There are spots in this book that are productive year-round. Yes, winter is definitely better than summer, but even during the summer I can still find an agate at some of the better sites.

Outgoing Tides

Outgoing tides agitate the rocks beds, pulling sand out to sea and expose the rock beds underneath. It's worthwhile to keep an eye on the tide charts and time your beach walks when tides are receding.

Mornings

I like to time my agate hunting with the outgoing tides if possible, but I have found that early morning hunts can be equally important to success. The ocean has had all night to do its thing and kick up fresh agates onto the beach, and I want to beat the crowds and be the first one out there looking regardless of the tides.

This is particularly important at the popular beaches that are close to town. If there are 20 people out there beachcombing in the same general area, you don't want to be the one that arrives hours late. Be the first person on the beach and you will be rewarded with more and better finds.

North Coast (Site Map)

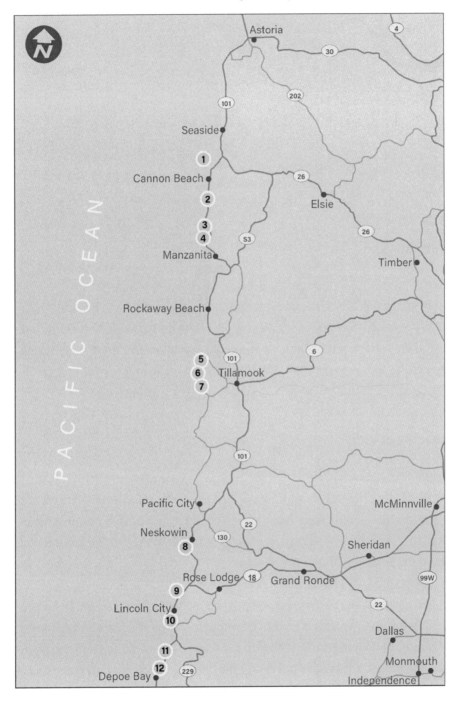

1. Indian Beach (Ecola State Park)

Directions:

Access to Indian Beach is relatively easy. From Cannon Beach, head north on Highway 101 a short distance and you will see signs for Ecola State Park just as you are leaving town. Entering the park, keep an eye out for the signs that lead you to Indian Beach. Note: This is a fee site requiring a parking pass.

Beachcombing:

Agate hunting has only been marginal the times that I have visited here, but it's worth mentioning since the northern coast has less agate hunting options than further south in Oregon, and this spot is still worth checking out if you are in the Seaside/Cannon Beach area.

This is a smaller beach that spans about 500 meters between Indian Point and Bald Point. On one recent visit in December, it turned up two large chunks of quartz that were worth adding to my collection. Walking from the main parking area south toward the end of the beach you will get into some rocky cliff and tide pool areas, but generally the results aren't too exciting.

Indian Beach is very popular during the summer, and being that it's a small beach is likely to get picked over quickly by visitors. Also be aware that the road into the beach is narrow and not suitable for large RVs or trailers. Parking can be limited during the summer as well. This site is best during the winter when there is much less activity.

Other Attractions:

While you are here, explore the rest of what Ecola State Park has to offer. There are many miles of beautiful hiking trails throughout the park, including an 8-mile stretch of the Oregon Coast Trail. The scenery here is incredible with impressive views of rocky shorelines and vast ocean expanses.

2. Arcadia Beach/Hug Point

Directions:

Both of these sites are a few miles south of Cannon Beach. Arcadia Beach (3.5 miles) and Hug Point (4.5 miles) both have access to parking right off Highway 101. Hug Point has bathrooms, while Arcadia Beach has no services. There are several more accesses to this stretch of the beach.

Beachcombing:

There is good access to long beaches here that you can walk for miles anywhere from Cannon Beach down to Hug Point.

Agate hunting here is very hit-or-miss in my experience. Most of the time you will find miles of sand with very little cobble, and attempting to find an agate or jasper can be pretty fruitless. However, if you time it just right and plan your visit after a good storm, this is an area known to produce an agate from time to time.

Other Attractions:

Cannon Beach is one of the more popular tourist towns along the coast and offers plenty of fun activities for the family. There is an impressive art community there with many galleries featuring glasswork, woodcarving, etc.

Definitely check out the Haystack Rock Marine Garden in Cannon Beach. This is a fascinating little ecosystem of tide pools that are exposed during low tide at Haystack Rock. There is an abundance of marine life that you can see up close in its natural environment. Just be aware that there is no collecting of any kind within the Marine Garden, which extends in a 300-yard radius from Haystack Rock.

3. Cove Beach

Directions:

To get there, turn west off Highway 101 on to Cove Beach Road. This turnoff is about 2 miles south of Arch Cape (1/2 mile south of the tunnel) or 6.5 miles north of Manzanita. Once on Cove Beach Road, drive for approximately 0.8 miles until you hit a "T". There is a small parking area to your right and a short trail to the beach. Parking area is only big enough for 2 or 3 vehicles.

Beachcombing:

This is a neat little access. It doesn't have any signage from the highway indicating access to the beach, and it is a decent distance away from the highway. There is no large parking area or services like many Oregon Coast beaches, so it is relatively unknown by most visitors to the coast. Definitely a nice spot to get away from the crowds at the more popular beaches.

I have had good luck agate hunting here. The beach has great cobble material to explore, with piles of round, black basalt stones piled up by the millions at the high tide line.

Low tide is always the best time to hunt for agates, but even during high tide you can explore these rock piles up high on the beach and find agates and jaspers hiding amongst them. Slowly walk through the black and grey rocks and keep your eyes peeled for anything that stands out. I found a big cream-colored agate several inches long that was just barely peeking out and only revealed its size after I did a bit of digging to expose it.

There is about 1.5 miles of good beach access here between Arch Cape and Cape Falcon.

Other Attractions:

The appeal of this area for me is the quiet and solitude. While you are still close to Cannon Beach, it has an isolated feel to it. The beach is basically surrounded by the Oswald West State Park which offers some great hiking opportunities.

4. Short Sand Beach (Oswald West)

Directions:

This isolated beach access is located south of Cape Falcon and north of Neahkahnie Mountain. Access to this beach requires a short hike, maybe 1/4 mile or so, down a nice paved trail to the beach. The hike is very easy and well suited for kids. There are restrooms available at the parking area as well as the beach. The parking area is on the east side of Highway 101 and well marked as Oswald West State Park.

Beachcombing:

The trail to the beach follows along Short Sand Creek to the beach access. There is about 1 mile of accessible sand beach to explore here.

Short Sand Creek and Necarney Creek both flow into the ocean at Short Sand Beach and provide good material for rockhounds. Even when the beaches are sanded up you can explore the creek and find good tumbler material in the creek bottom.

I have found some nice agates, jasper and "jasp-agate" pieces at Short Sand

Beach. Some impressive wave action can occur on this beach making it a popular site for surfers, but those same waves can bring up some nice material for us agate hunters too!

Other Attractions:

On the walk into Short Sand Beach, you will see a sign for "Old Growth Trail." This will take you on a beautiful hike through some spectacular old growth spruce, cedar, hemlock, and fir trees. The inaccessibility of this area back in the day deterred loggers in many parts of Oswald West State Park, leaving behind these old treasures for us to enjoy today.

Other hiking trails within the park will lead you to explore Cape Falcon and Neahkahnie Mountain.

Good gravels at the mouth of Short Sand Creek.

5. Cape Meares

Directions:

Cape Meares is a neat little coastal town located on the west side of Tillamook Bay. From Tillamook, head west on Highway 131 for about 2 miles. Just as the road makes a wide bend to the south, turn right on Bayocean Rd NW. Follow the road along Tillamook Bay all the way to the town of Cape Meares. Beach can be accessed right in town.

Beachcombing:

This spot will get you access to several miles of beach from Cape Meares and many miles all the way up the Bayocean Peninsula.

Cape Meares is a nice little beach town that seems more isolated than many on the coast, and therefore doesn't get near the traffic from beachcombers. It is a known agate producing stretch of beach with good material to search. You can find agates, jaspers and interesting zeolite specimens here. I have had particularly good luck walking south of town toward to rocky cliffs and usually find better materials to search there, although anywhere can be good when the conditions are right.

There is a known fossil site along Bayocean Road as you are driving along Tillamook Bay on your way to Cape Meares. Look for exposed sandstone cliffs along the bay; these are ancient seabeds that contain a variety of different marine fossils.

While you are in Cape Meares, make sure you also do some hunting at Short Beach (site #6) just north of Oceanside. This is one of my favorite agate hunting sites in Oregon and definitely should not be missed.

Other Attractions:

The Cape Meares Lighthouse provides some excellent views. It is a great site for whale watching. It is surrounded by the Cape Meares National Wildlife Refuge which is home to many seabirds and other marine life. Bring your binoculars!

6. Short Beach

Directions:

Short Beach is tucked away just south of Cape Meares State Park and north of Oceanside. Access to Short Beach can be found approximately 1 mile north of Oceanside. Roadside parking is permitted immediately before Radar Road. Keep a sharp eye out, it's easy to miss!

Beachcombing:

Don't let the mere 1,000 meter span of Short Beach fool you...this hidden gem is packed with treasures, most notably agates, jaspers, and zeolites.

There is a rustic stepped pathway leading down to the beach with plenty of benches to stop and rest and take in the majestic scenery, reminiscent of an Ursula le Guin novel. It's a short hike to the beach, though separated enough from the road that it feels like your very own private beach. If you walk north across the creek you will find some quality cobbled area and plenty of good agates. The flume waterfall adds to the scenery. It's worth taking a picnic lunch and spending the afternoon here.

Exploring further south, closer to the cliff wall, there are some small zeolites hidden in the rocks. If you muster the courage to cross over the cliff wall you'll find a sea cave. Be wary of sneaker waves if you cross over into this area. Short Beach is extremely private, with plenty of untouched areas to explore. You're best bet is going to be exploring the cobbled beach area, but don't neglect rockier areas in your search.

Other Attractions:

Oceanside is 1 mile south of Short Beach, with more good beach access, motels, and plenty of small cafes for recharging or unwinding. There is a pet friendly hotel right on the beach, but don't go to Oceanview if you're looking for nightlife. It's a sleepy little town, perfect for a quiet home base as you expand outward in your agate hunting adventures.

A dandy little orange agate found on a sunny day at Short Beach.

This is what you are hoping to see... gravel beds spread far and wide...

Big clear agates found at Short Beach.

7. Oceanside Beach

Directions:

The Oceanside Beach Recreation Area is located right in the small town of Oceanside. From Tillamook, take Highway 131 west about 9 miles. Access to the beach is right in town and has plenty of parking and restrooms.

Beachcombing:

This is one of the better agate hunting locations on the north coast. Generally I have found better material if you hike north toward the rocks (Maxwell Point), although anywhere between Oceanside and Netarts can be good on the right day.

If you hunt closer to Maxwell Point, you can then venture over to a little "hidden gem" known as Tunnel Beach. It is accessible by a small man made tunnel that goes through the rocks. The tunnel is short, but it's still not a bad idea to bring a flashlight with you so you can negotiate over the slippery rocks.

On the other side, you will generally be rewarded with some nice agate hunting at Tunnel Beach. There is usually a lot more rocky material here than there is down by Oceanside and Netarts. Agates, jaspers and zeolites can be abundant here on the right day.

On very rare occasions you can also search Lost Boy Beach, which is north of Tunnel Beach and south of Short Beach. Access is better if you start at Short Beach and go south. However, timing with the low tide is critical (-1.5 to -2.0). Most days it is inaccessible. Do not attempt it if you are unsure.

Other Attractions:

Drive a few miles north on Highway 131 and you're at Cape Meares Lighthouse. Impressive vistas overlook the rocky coastline and hidden beaches in this secluded stretch of the Oregon Coast. This is a great site for whale watching.

If you're feeling adventurous, you can head down to Netarts Bay and try your hand at crabbing and clamming. Local marinas offer equipment rentals and can teach you the basics. A super fun activity for kids!

A pair of beachcombers looking for agates on the beach at Oceanside.

8. Neskowin Beach

Directions:

Neskowin is a nice little coastal town north of Lincoln City about 13 miles just off Highway 101. This town seems to have embraced a quieter atmosphere, and although it does have a few businesses it doesn't get overrun with tourists like some other coast towns do in the summer.

There is a large parking area immediately when you turn off Highway 101. Park there and take the path that follows along the creek to the beach.

Beachcombing:

I have found good material close to town. Go at low tide and explore around Proposal Rock for a variety of different beach treasures. I found some nice pieces without much effort on my last visit, and was also rewarded with a nice intact sand dollar and a few other shells too.

If you aren't finding much, you can walk north along the beach for a good distance. There are some other beach access points in Neskowin if you drive through town. Go north on Breaker Avenue (the road closest to the ocean) for about 1/2 mile and you will find another small parking area.

Sometimes there are seals in the little cove at Hawk Creek. Be sure to keep your distance and make sure your dogs are leashed up if you see them in the area.

Other Attractions:

A short 5-mile drive north on Highway 101 and you will arrive at the Nestucca Bay National Wildlife Refuge. It is a bird watcher's paradise, with a wide variety of different species, particularly waterfowl and shorebirds. It's not uncommon to spot blacktail deer, Roosevelt elk, and other larger critters if you keep an eye out.

It's never a bad day on the Oregon Coast...

9. Road's End

Directions:

This is an easy access at the north end of Lincoln City. To get there, turn on Logan Road off Highway 101 (near the casino). Drive about 1 mile north and you will reach the Road's End access. There are plenty of signs to get you there.

This is a nice day-use area with restrooms and picnic tables, and several miles of beach access in both directions.

Beachcombing:

Since this site is located right in Lincoln City it is a popular beach access. Fortunately there is some good material here for us beachcombers. You can hunt anywhere on the beach, but the best spot is a bit of a hike to the north.

The first thing you will want to check are the tide charts, because the best spot is only accessible during low tide. Head north about 1 mile from the parking area toward the cliffs and "God's Thumb." When the tides are low you should be able to scramble around the rocks and get to a small hidden cove.

This cove is no secret to agate hunters, but it gets a lot less visitors than the main beach near the parking area. It also has much better materials most of the time, with abundant cobble material to search through. Nice agates from clear, yellow, and even orange carnelian agates can be found here. Various green, yellow, and red jaspers are relatively easy to find, and even an occasional petrified wood can be spotted.

This spot requires some scrambling over rocks so be prepared, and as mentioned already be sure you are aware of the tides charts so you can get back to the main beach before the ocean starts rising.

Usually we do our beachcombing near the water's edge, but Lincoln City also has glass floats to find! Each year, glass artists in Lincoln City scatter roughly 3,000 fancy glass floats on the beaches for visitors to find anywhere from Road's End down to Siletz Bay. To find them, look up above the beach amongst the grasses and driftwood.

Other Attractions:

Since this site is located right in Lincoln City, one of Oregon's most popular coastal towns, there are lots of fun "touristy" things to check out; art galleries, bookstores, casinos, and of course, plenty of good food to eat.

10. Nelscott Beach

Directions:

You will have no trouble finding access to Nelscott Beach, as it runs along the southern part of Lincoln City between D River and the Siletz River. One easy access is the public beach access on 35th Street, but there are many other access points throughout town that are well marked.

Beachcombing:

Nelscott Beach is very popular since it is right in Lincoln City. This is also one of the closest agate hunting sites from Portland, so you will definitely see plenty of beachcombers while you are here.

I haven't had the best luck at Nelscott Beach. It is certainly a very popular place to look for agates, and if you time it right then the agate hunting can be as good as anywhere, but most of the times I have been there it is always sanded up and unproductive.

Nevertheless, I am very confident to include it here in this book because it is most definitely a known agate site. For whatever reason, my trips here haven't been very productive, but I have friends who have come to Nelscott Beach and found handfuls of dandy agates and jaspers. As always, timing is everything when you are beachcombing on the coast.

Remember that Lincoln City hides decorative glass floats on the beaches above the high tide line. They can be found anywhere along the 7 mile stretch between Roads End and Siletz Bay. Search carefully amongst the driftwood and grasses.

Other Attractions:

There are several hundred resident harbor seals that live in Siletz Bay and feed on the abundance of fish in this marine estuary. Bring your binoculars and see if you can spot them resting along the bay.

This little blood-red agate was the prize of the day!

11. Gleneden Beach

Directions:

Gleneden Beach is located approximately 5.5 miles north of Depoe Bay and 7 miles south of Lincoln City. Easy access to the beach can be found at the Gleneden Beach State Park that is accessed by turning on Westler Road off Highway 101. There is good signage to the parking area.

The last time I visited this site, erosion had broken up the trail that goes from the parking area to the beach making it somewhat challenging to get down. Not to worry, if you have difficulty getting to the beach here, there are many other access points throughout the area. Go back out to Highway 101 and go north into the town of Gleneden Beach. You should have no trouble finding the beach.

Beachcombing:

The productivity of this site will vary a lot depending on the weather. Whenever I visited during the summer it was mostly sanded up and difficult to find much. As usual, you can increase your odds of finding good material by timing your agate hunt when the tide is heading out. At low tide you will have the best luck.

During prime beach agate hunting season in winter and early spring, Gleneden Beach can be quite productive with a nice variety of agates and jaspers, along with the occasional fossil turning up.

From Gleneden Beach you can meander your way north to Salishan Beach (a 2 mile long sand spit) and continue your agate hunt. Most road accesses along this stretch of beach are private so you will need to hike to get there, but this is a good way to get away from the crowds.

If you don't have any luck finding agates at Gleneden Beach, I recommend taking a short 3 mile drive south on Highway 101 to Fogarty Creek State Recreation Area. This is a very good beach for agates and jaspers that always seems to turn up a few treasures for me, even during the "off season."

Other Attractions:

Siletz Bay is also a great spot to do some clamming. If you've never dug clams before, just visit one of the local sporting good stores and they will get you all set up. It's actually pretty easy once you figure out how to do it, and it's another great family activity you can do (just like agate hunting) that doesn't cost you much money that is loads of fun.

12. Fogarty Creek

Directions:

The Fogarty Creek State Recreation Area is a very popular access right off Highway 101, approximately 3 miles north of Depoe Bay. You will see two signs indicating a North Fogarty Creek and South Fogarty Creek. Both accesses will get you to the beach. There is no camping available here, but there is a very nice picnicking area, restrooms, and plenty of parking. To access the beach, follow the trail that follows Fogarty Creek and goes underneath the highway.

In spite of its easy access, Fogarty Beach has a nice feeling of being secluded and is a great place to spend the day.

Beachcombing:

Fogarty Beach is one of my favorite places on the Oregon Coast to hunt for agates. It is a beautiful small beach, and I never fail to find some good pieces when I visit here. Unlike many Oregon beaches that can really "sand up" in the summertime, Fogarty Beach usually has some nice cobble material that will contain abundant agates and jaspers.

Fogarty Creek enters the Pacific Ocean here, and if you are willing to get your feet wet then there is some good materials right in the creek itself. There is only a few hundred feet of beach south of the creek before you hit some cliffs, but this short stretch of beach will usually produce. You will find some pretty little jaspers here that are quite small, sometimes the size of a pea or smaller. A good place for the kids to use their keen eyes!

Venturing north provides some good access, but the beach gets very narrow as you walk north, so be aware of the tides and watch out for sneaker waves that could push you into the rocks. If conditions seem at all dangerous, stick to the main beach.

I have found some nice complete clams here, and there are usually some decent fossils to be found if you keep your eyes peeled.

Since this is a popular beach, I recommend that you time your agate hunting with the tides, and consider coming early in the morning before the crowds have picked it over too hard.

Other Attractions:

You'd be missing out if you didn't stop at the Boiler Bay State Scenic Viewpoint. This has got to be one of Oregon's most epic viewpoints, a rugged, rocky bay surrounded by basalt cliffs.

Bring your binoculars and enjoy watching a variety of seabirds that call Boiler Bay their home. At low tide you can spot remnants of a shipwreck from 1910. This is also one of the best spots along the coast for whale watching.

A nice handful of small, colorful jaspers found at Fogarty Beach.

Central Coast (Site Map)

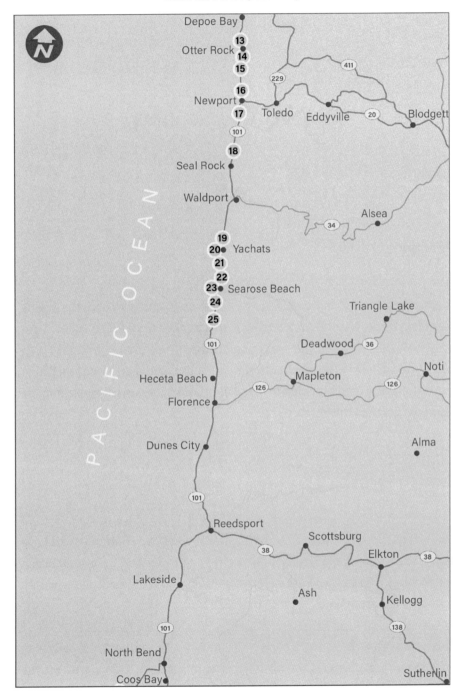

13. Devil's Punchbowl

Directions:

This access is located approximately 5.5 miles south of Depoe Bay at the Devil's Punchbowl State Natural Area. Access is well marked from Highway 101. Turn west on Otter Crest Loop and again on 1st Street. There is a large parking area and restroom just before you reach the end of the road. Look for a small sign marked "Beach Trail" that leads you to a wooden staircase that goes roughly 100 steps down to the beach.

Beachcombing:

You will quickly hit cliffs to the north, but if you head south you will have access to a long 5-mile stretch of beach that continues on to Beverly Beach and Moolack Beach. If you are feeling ambitious you could walk all the way to Yaquina Head from here.

This beach is a well-known agate producer. When I come here, I usually plan on going for a good hike. I usually find better material by hiking farther to the south. If the beaches are heavily sanded when you visit and lack much in the way of cobbles, you may have a hard time finding agates. In this case, I would recommend you venture south to either Beverly Beach or Moolack Beach.

Fossils are commonly found on the beach at the Devil's Punchbowl access. These fossils are sourced from what Is called the "Astoria Formation," an ancient sea floor that became exposed during a period of geological uplift some 15 to 20 million years ago. The sea cliffs just south of the staircase leading down to the beach are an example of the Astoria formation that extends south all the way to Yaquina Head.

These exposed cliffs are sandstones that contain a wide variety of fossils. Most common are invertebrates (clams, snails, etc.). Dozens of different species have been identified from this formation. While hunting for agates keep your eyes open for nice fossil specimens as well. It isn't too difficult to find complete fossil clams, and concretions that contain broken shell fragments are very common here.

Other Attractions:

Of course, you would be missing out if you didn't see the Devil's Punchbowl while you are here. You can't see it from the beach access described above; you'll need to go back up the stairs and go to the end of 1st Street to the overlook. This unique geologic feature is unlike any other along the coast.

14. Beverly Beach

Directions:

Beverly Beach is approximately 6 miles north of Newport and 7 miles south of Depoe Bay. Look for the turnoff for Beverly Beach State Park. Access is on the east side of Highway 101 with a path that goes underneath the highway to the beach. There is plenty of parking along with camping and RV access. There are also some large pull outs along the highway where you can access the beach.

Beachcombing:

If you visit in the summer, this beach will most likely be sanded up with little in the way of agates. Timing is critical here because the agate hunting can actually be quite good if you time it well. A visit during the wintertime can be very productive. Hunt around the mouth of Spencer Creek if gravels are present.

Abundant fossils are sourced from what is known as the Astoria Formation, an ancient seashore dating back 15 - 20 million years that is exposed along the sea cliffs in the area. A variety of different fossils can be found here, including various bivalve and gastropod fossils (clams and snails). While complete pieces are sometimes found, most commonly you will find shell fragments within concretions of sandstone matrix. Vertebrate fossils (whale, seal and dolphin bones, shark teeth, etc.) have also been found, although much rarer.

Take the path under the highway and follow the cliffs to the south. You will start to notice seashells and other marine fossils embedded in the sandstone. It is illegal to dig into these cliffs but don't worry, you should be able to find plenty of loose fossil specimens scattered around the beach in this area.

Other Attractions:

Check out the fascinating "ghost forest stump" located right at the parking area at Beverly Beach. There are actually lots of these well-preserved "ghost forests" all along the Oregon Coast but they are rarely seen.

So how did they form? At some point in history the conditions along the coast caused sections of forest to be swallowed up by beach sands. Being covered in sand and water, an anaerobic environment was created with prevented decay. Carbon dating dates them anywhere from 1,000 to 7,000 years in age. Periodically, violent storms will strip away sands and expose these ancient stumps once again.

A large chunk of ancient sea bed that has eroded from the hillside. Smaller fossil specimens are common at both Beverly Beach and Moolack Beach.

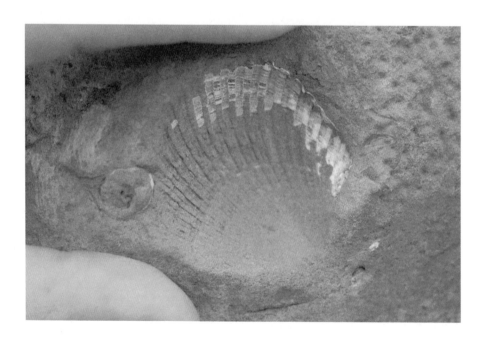

15. Moolack Beach

Directions:

Moolack Beach is approximately 4.5 miles north of Newport and 8.5 miles south of Depoe Bay. The beach is easily accessed by a large pullout right off the west side of Highway 101. Keep an eye out for the signs. The proximity of Moolack Beach to both Newport and Depoe Bay makes it a very popular beach during the summer.

Beachcombing:

Moolack Beach offers lots of fun things for the beachcomber. In addition to being a productive beach for agate hunting, there is also an abundance of fossils that are commonly found here.

This beach can vary quite a bit depending on the weather and time of year. Storms do a good job of stirring up material and exposing rocks on the surface. During the summer, beaches are generally more sandy making agates less abundant.

I have had good luck exploring two of the creeks that flow into the ocean nearby. Walk a few hundred feet south of the parking area and you will see Moolack Creek. A few hundred feet north of the parking area is Coal Creek. There is usually some quality cobble materials to hunt in the creeks, including nice jaspers and agates. This is a good place to check if you aren't finding much along the beach itself.

Just like on Beverly Beach, there are abundant fossils here. Ancient seashores are exposed at various points along the sea cliffs in this area. If you are up for the hike, you can get there by starting at Moolack Beach and walking north. Walk along the cliffs as you go, and soon you will start noticing small white fossils embedded in the sandstone.

Collecting invertebrate fossils is allowed along the coast, but keep in mind that it is illegal to dig into the cliff walls. Not a problem though, as the ocean waves do a fine job of eroding the cliffs all by themselves, and there are plenty of fossils scattered along the beach that you can pick up. Vertebrate fossils cannot be collected without a permit in Oregon.

Other Attractions:

This is a good access point with several miles of beach to explore. Looking south you will see the beautiful and picturesque Yaquina Head Lighthouse. A long sandy beach stretches all the way from Yaquina Head to Devil's Punchbowl State Natural Area providing many miles of good beach access, with plenty of pull outs along Highway 101.

If the fossils have piqued your interest, be sure to visit the Hatfield Marine Science Center in Newport. It is one of the leading marine research laboratories in the U.S. They have a Visitor Center that is open seven days a week during the summer months. This is also a great place to bring in your fossil finds if you would like help with identification.

16. Agate Beach

Directions:

The access at Agate Beach is approximately 1.5 miles north of Newport. A small parking area accessible from NW Oceanview Drive goes right along the beach. If the small parking lot along the road is full, there is plenty more parking available at the Agate Beach State Recreation Area. There is clear signage off Highway 101 to the Rec Area.

Beachcombing:

This beach is usually a little less picked over than the accesses right in Nye Beach and Newport. The beach is a central location that provides access that stretches all the way from Yaquina Head Outstanding Natural Area to the jetty at Yaquina Bay in Newport.

The beaches around Newport are well-known for being rich agate producers, and certainly the name Agate Beach indicates this to be the case. However, this spot may be better reserved for the winter months, when heavy storms and wave action tend to expose materials. During the summer months agates seem to be less abundant here, with lots of sand and much less in the way of cobble materials to hunt. The occasional agate will still show up in the sands though, if you spend enough time looking. Always be on the lookout for rocks, shell fragments, and other material washed up by the surf. This is where the agates will be.

Other Attractions:

Don't pass up the Yaquina Head Outstanding Natural Area. The lighthouse at Yaquina Head is the tallest in Oregon, but in my eyes the amazing tide pools are the real attraction here.

Visiting during low tide offers a look at a truly fascinating ecosystem. This area is managed by the Bureau of Land Management with an Interpretive Center featuring exhibits on seabird and other marine life.

17. South Beach

Directions:

This is an easy access just south of Newport. The easiest access is approximately 3 miles south of downtown Newport. Look for signs indicating South Beach State Park right off Highway 101. There is a large parking area and restroom available at this site.

There are many miles of beach to explore at this site. From the South Jetty at Yaquina Bay down past the Newport Airport is all worth exploring.

Beachcombing:

It's no secret that the beaches of Newport are some of the best agate hunting in Oregon. In fact, some consider this to be one of the premier agate hunting locations on the Pacific Coast, with a wide variety of agates ranging from small pieces up to rare chunks weighing several pounds being found every year!

Of course, Newport is one of the most popular towns along the Oregon coast, so there is no shortage of agate hunters here. Not to worry though, there are plenty of agates for everyone! Winter storms and the never-ending tides alway bring in new fresh agates for collectors to enjoy.

Still, this is a good time to encourage you to collect just enough agates to whet your appetite, and leave a few for other beachcombers. Also keep in mind that there is a limit of 1-gallon per day collecting rule along the Oregon coast. That is a whole lot of agates, but it isn't too difficult to collect that many if you go out at low tide, particularly after a good angry winter storm!

This is also one of the best areas to search for the rare "Newport Blues," a dark blue agate that is highly valued by collectors. These can be a dark, almost grey/black color and are easy to miss if you aren't careful. So keep a sharp eye out for these beautiful agates. They take a nice polish and are a real trophy for the rockhound. Black, pink, and other fancy agates can be found all around Newport.

Be on the lookout for petrified wood as well. These are often tumbled into smooth stones that will blend in with other rocks, but close inspection will show banding and the tell-tale "rings" indicating an ancient piece of petrified wood.

Fossils are also plentiful here. A wide array of invertebrate fossils can be collected along the beaches at Newport. Vertebrate fossils such as whale and seal bones are much less common, but they are found from time to time. Collection of vertebrate fossils is not allowed without a permit. If you think you have found one, it should be reported to the Hatfield Marine Science Center in Newport.

Other Attractions:

There is no shortage of interesting sites to see in Newport. I highly recommend a visit to the Oregon Coast Aquarium. The Hatfield Marine Science Center also has a Visitor's Center that is a very interesting place to visit. And finally, after a long day of agate hunting, consider stopping for a drink at the Rogue Brewery.

18. Ona Beach

Directions:

Ona Beach is approximately 9 miles south of Newport and 7 miles north of Waldport. Access is right off Highway 101 and well-marked. There is a large parking area and nice nature trail to the beach which crosses Beaver Creek.

This site gives you several miles of great beach access in each direction.

Beachcombing:

Ona Beach is right in the heart of prime agate hunting. I recommend walking south along the seashore toward Seal Rock. There are about 2 miles of prime area to search for beachcombing.

This part of the coast is one of the best sites to agate hunt in the entire state. Not only are agates abundant here, but there is a nice variety of different types available to the collector, including rare varieties of blue and black agate.

Jaspers are abundant in a variety of colors along this beach, ranging from reds and yellows, to brown and green colors. Jaspers are an opaque variety of silica that are very hard (6.5 – 7 on the Mohs scale) and have different colors depending on the impurities within the stone. Iron inclusions within the stone can be credited for the reddish color that is commonly seen.

I have also found more than a few "jasp-agates" along this stretch of beach, in which a piece shows characteristics of both jasper and agate within the same stone. Some of these can be particularly beautiful and are a favorite of mine.

Fossils are also abundant along this beach. Clam fossils that have eroded from the Astoria Formation are commonly washed up along this beach. Shell fragments and conglomerate pieces are most common, but occasionally you will also find a nice complete piece to add to your collection.

There is usually some decent material here at any time of the year, but prime agate hunting season is definitely the time to come. Usually anytime during winter or early spring is good. Low tide is always best, and if you can time your hunt with one of the brutal storms that often hits the coast this time of year, you may find a real bounty of beautiful agates and jaspers at this site.

Other attractions:

Just 2 miles south is the town of Seal Rock, a lovely little beach town that get a bit less tourist activity than nearby Newport. At Seal Rock State Park you can explore beautiful tide pools and you might catch a glimpse of an occasional harbor seal.

There are also several art galleries worth checking out in Seal Rock, including blown glass art, wood carvings, and more.

19. Smelt Sands

Directions:

The Smelt Sands access is a short distance north of downtown Yachats. From the bridge across the Yachats River, drive north on Highway 101 for about a mile. You will see a sign at Sunset Road at the turnoff to Smelt Sands State Park.

This is a typical state park access with a restroom, small picnic area and enough parking for about 10 vehicles. There is a nice path that follows above the rocky shoreline. Access can be found on small beaches in between the coarse basalt flows that jut out into the ocean. The beach looks a little different each time you visit here, but you can almost always find some good gravel to search.

Beachcombing:

My family has been coming to Yachats for many years. It is one of the most beautiful (and dangerous) stretches of the Oregon Coast, famous for its monstrous waves that come crashing into the rocky shorelines. People make special trips here during stormy weather just to catch a glimpse of these world-class waves.

For the agate hunter, this site is just about as close to a "sure thing" as you will find. I have been here a dozen times or more, and have never been skunked at Smelt Sands. It is no secret that Yachats has some of the best agate pickin' on the entire coast.

There are almost always small sized agates and jaspers here. Most often they are tiny little bits ranging from pea-sized to jelly bean-sized agates, but they are abundant and you can easily fill your pockets with beautiful little treasures in an array of colors.

There are big rock points that extend out into the ocean and they might seem tempting to walk out on, but if you fall into the ocean there is literally nowhere to climb out due to vertical rock walls. Many people have died at this exact spot, so give it the respect that it deserves.

Other Attractions:

My dad and I always do some surf fishing here and have done quite well over the years. With the right setup and a little bit of patience, you can almost always catch some sea perch at this spot. The local hardware store in Yachats carries some basic fishing gear and can give you advice on how to catch them. Not only are they fun to catch, but they also taste pretty good too!

There are always reliable gravel at Smelt Sands. I've never gotten skunked here.

Tiny treasures from a short hunt at Smelt Sands.

20. Yachats

Directions:

In downtown Yachats just north of the river, turn west on Ocean View Drive to get to the Yachats State Recreation Site. You can park at the designated parking area and walk north along Ocean View Drive to access several small gravelly beaches.

Beachcombing:

This is another excellent site to explore. Similar to Smelt Sands, you can scramble down to the beaches and almost always find some nice agates hidden amongst the rocky shore. They are usually jelly bean-sized and smaller, but they are abundant. You will almost never go home empty handed in Yachats.

There is more good access to the coastline on the other side of the river. Go back to Highway 101 and look for Yachats Ocean Road immediately south of the bridge across the river. It follows along the shore for about 1/2 mile providing several spots to check out. Some spots are too rocky for agate hunting, but you can often find small pockets where gravel collects that will hold some treasures.

I know it may get redundant, but this is yet another location that deserves a special note about the dangers of sneaker waves. Even on the calmest of days, the rocky shoreline here can create some waves that will surprise you. This is one site where you need to be especially cautious, particularly if you have children with you.

Other Attractions:

The Yachats Agate Festival is a celebration of the beautiful agate treasures found in this tiny coastal town. It occurs every winter (usually in January, but the dates change every year). Many vendors are there selling a variety of gems and minerals. There are also talks and demonstrations about rockhounding and lapidary. This is usually a great time of year to come to Yachats and enjoy the epic waves!

Time in Yachats always results in some nice treasures...

21. Neptune Beach

Directions:

From Yachats, drive south on Highway 101 for approximately 3.8 miles. The parking area for Neptune State Scenic Viewpoint is right off the highway. Go another 1/4 mile or so and you will find another small parking area just south of Cummins Creek.

Beachcombing:

The beaches between Yachats and Florence are probably the best agate hunting on the central coast. Agate hunters go out of their way to hit these beaches because they can be so productive. Neptune Beach is one of the best.

This is a long sandy shoreline with lots of cobbles to search. Even in the summertime when beachcombing can be less productive I can usually find at least a few agates here. I usually find more agates in Yachats than I do at this site, but not always. If you time it right, Neptune Beach can be exceptional hunting.

If you are having trouble finding any good material here, do some poking around at the mouth of Cummins Creek. All of the creeks in this area consistently produce some high quality agates and jasper material.

Other Attractions:

Thor's Well is a fascinating natural phenomenon about a mile north of Neptune Beach and south of Cape Perpetua. Some call it the "Drainpipe of the Pacific." It is actually a big hole that seems like it sucks in seawater like a giant flushing toilet. Time your visit with high tide for the best show.

22. Strawberry Hill

Directions:

From Yachats, drive south on Highway 101 for 5 miles. The parking area for Strawberry Hill Wayside is right off the highway. The small parking area isn't particularly well suited for RVs. Access down to the beach is a bit of a descent, but you will be rewarded with some excellent hunting.

Beachcombing:

This site is one of the hidden gems of the Oregon Coast, easily missed as you drive down the highway. It's a favorite with the locals.

This is one beach where it is especially worth visiting at low tide. The tide pools here are as good as anywhere on the coast, perhaps even better than the more famous sites popular with tourists. Here there are way less people, and the variety of marine life is spectacular. Starfish, mussels, crabs, anemones and seals. The sea life here is amazing.

As for agate hunting... well lets just keep it simple. **This is easily one of the best sites on the coast, and a worthwhile spot to visit anytime of the year.** I have found some very large agates here, and even on the rare occasion that I don't find anything I am always happy I came. So beautiful here.

23. Bob's Creek

Directions:

From Yachats, drive south on Highway 101 for 5.7 miles and look for the Bob's Creek Wayside. The creek enters the ocean here and access to the beach is easy, but the parking area is small and can fill up quickly, so try to get here early in the morning.

Beachcombing:

This is another rough, rocky beach that is one of the most productive on the entire coast. If you've got the time and really want to find some agates, the stretch of coastline starting at Yachats and going down 10 miles or so are the best. Bob's is just about as good as it gets.

Agate hunting here is fantastic. It's also no secret amongst hardcore agate hunters, and many people drive hours just to hunt these gravel beds. This is a site that I would recommend researching the tide charts and try to visit early in the morning when the tides are down. You should be rewarded nicely.

There's no bad spot to look here. The mouth of Bob's Creek it right at the parking area on the north end of Bob's Beach. There is always some good gravel here that you can explore. You can continue north for a few hundred feet, but eventually it cliffs out. Head south, and you can walk for 1/3 of a mile before hitting more cliffs. This stretch of beach is usually full of nice gravel and plenty of agates. I could spend all day zig-zagging this beach.

This is no sandy walk on the beach, so come prepared with good footwear and be ready to explore. The tide pools here are amazing. This is easily one of my favorite sites in this book just for that alone. Keep an eye out for harbor seals as they swim around the jagged rocks. They are often curious and will come closer than you might expect.

Beachcombers looking for agates at the mouth of Bob's Creek.

Gorgeous jasp-agate found at Bob's Creek Wayside.

24. Stonefield Beach

Directions:

From Yachats, drive south on Highway 101 for approximately 7 miles. A large parking area is just prior to the Tenmile Creek bridge. Cross the bridge and there is an even smaller parking spot just south of the Creek. No facilities at this site.

Beachcombing:

This is another very good site for agate hunters. My last trip here was relatively unproductive with just a few jaspers to show for my efforts. However, I have also had some days here when the beachcombing was as good as I have ever had on the coast.

This is definitely a beach that is worth the drive. It is a popular spot for agate hunters from Florence, but lots of people from Eugene, Portland, and all around the state make the drive to hunt for agates. If the gravel beds are exposed then you can expect some excellent hunting at Stonefield Beach.

There is often some good material in Tenmile Creek right by the parking area.

If you aren't having much luck here, try walking south for 1/4 mile, and the beach gets rockier. Get away from the sand and you will likely find some better material.

Other Attractions:

One of the many beautiful lighthouses on the Oregon Coast is found at Heceta Head, 13 miles south of Yachats. Many consider this to be the most beautiful lighthouse on the coast, and I've also heard that it is the most photographed lighthouse in the United States.

This is also a popular site for whale watching, as grey whales make their migration from Baja to Alaska. There is a day use fee at the Heceta Head Lighthouse State Scenic Viewpoint.

25. Roosevelt Beach

Directions:

From Florence, head north on Highway 101 for about 14 miles. One handy access is at the Carl G. Washburn Memorial State Park. The other is about 3/4 miles north at the Muriel O. Ponsler Memorial State Park. Both accesses are good, but Washburn is a bigger parking area and usually has more people.

Beachcombing:

I found my biggest and best agate at Roosevelt Beach on one weekend trip that I took to the Central Oregon Coast.

The abundance of agates in this stretch of beach is likely credited to the numerous creeks that drain onto the beach here, continuously washing out new materials that have washed back up on the shores. China Creek is right at the Muriel O. Ponsler access. Walk 1/2 mile north and you can search around the mouth of Big Creek. From the Carl G. Washburn access, walk south about 1/4 mile and search around Blowout Creek.

If the conditions are right, you will find gravel everywhere and you will have no trouble collecting abundant agates and jaspers. But if beaches are sanded up and hunting is difficult, then searching around the mouths of these creeks can mean the difference between success and going home empty-handed.

Other Attractions:

The Sea Lion Caves are one of the most popular attractions on the Oregon Coast. Located about 11 miles north of Florence, it is the largest natural sea cave in America. It is home to a healthy group of Stellar sea lions, whose population averages around 200 or so. The sea lions come and go as they please, feeding on various species of fish and squid. This is a privately-owned operation and does require tickets to see, but it's definitely worth the visit if you've never seen it.

Just about back to the parking lot after a long hike, I looked down in the sand and was greeted with this bright, beautiful agate. Wow!

South Coast (Site Map)

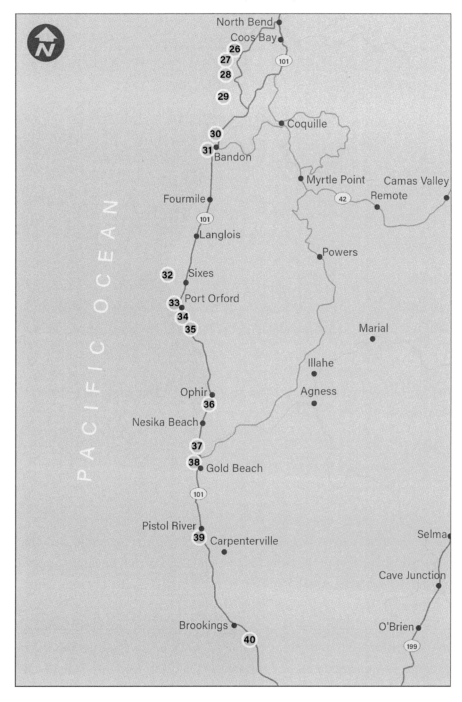

26. Sunset Bay

Directions:

Turn off Highway 101 at North Bend and head past the town of Charleston. Take the Cape Arago Highway about 2.5 miles past Charleston to get to Sunset Bay State Park.

There are good waves in this area and you will likely see a few surfers while you are here. There are restrooms and nice picnic areas as well.

Beachcombing:

This is a beautiful narrow bay with towering basalt cliffs on each side. You can follow along the sides of the cliffs for a way if you want, but be careful not to get yourself in a bad situation. Always remember that large waves can come at unexpected times.

Big Creek enters on the south end of Sunset Bay, and I have always found the best gravel around the mouth of the creek. On my last few visits, the beach was mostly all sand except for a few hundred feet of good gravel right around the mouth of Big Creek.

If you strike out at Sunset Bay, you can try your luck at Yoakam Point, which is about a mile back toward Charleston. It is easy to miss but there is a small parking area and trail that leads to the beach.

Other Attractions:

Head past Sunset Bay for another mile and you will find Shore Acres State Park. There is a Japanese-style botanical garden here that is quite beautiful, and if you visit between Thanksgiving and New Years (prime agate season!) they have an impressive holiday light display here. There is a small parking fee at this site.

Red jaspers like these are common all along the Oregon Coast.

27. Simpson Reef

Directions:

Turn off Highway 101 at North Bend and head past the town of Charleston. Take the Cape Arago Highway about 5 miles past Charleston to arrive at the Simpson Reef Overlook. This access is not for the faint of heart! It requires a treacherous hike and I would not recommend it for children or if you have mobility issues. The hike down is quite steep with a rope cable to hold on to.

Beachcombing:

There is an excellent rocky stretch of coastline that goes from Shore Acres State Park down to the Simpson Reef south to North Cove. Much of this section is completely inaccessible with steep towering cliffs.

This rough, rugged shoreline makes for some exceptional waves that draw quite a few surfers to the area and there are several access trails that go down to the ocean from the Cape Arago Highway.

The trail I took was right at the Simpson Reef Overlook. It's not an obvious access, but you can scramble around the parking lot and there is a trail that drops down to the beach below. **This is a much harder access than most in this book**, but it's usually worth it. The shoreline is completely loaded with gravel that turn up lots of great agates. Since the access is difficult, the beaches get hunted way less than most others and the potential for good finds is excellent. However, if the trail seems intimidating then I encourage you to find an alternate site.

Other Attractions:

If you enjoy viewing wildlife then you should take a detour and visit the South Slough National Estuary Research Reserve. Head back toward Charleston, and turn south on Seven Devils Road just as you enter town. Go another 5 miles or so for the main access. This is a 5900-acre preserve with a wide diversity of plants, fish and birds. Several businesses in the area offer kayak rentals.

28. Cape Arago

Directions:

Turn off Highway 101 at North Bend and head past the town of Charleston. Take the Cape Arago Highway about 5.5 miles to arrive at Cape Arago State Park (the end of the road.)

This is another access that starts high above the ocean at a spectacular vista, which means you will need to hike down trails to get to the beach.

Beachcombing:

This general area is excellent for agate hunting for a few reasons. For one thing, it is one of the least accessible parts of the Oregon Coast. From Bandon to Coos Bay, Highway 101 goes inland away from the beaches and there are many miles of the coast that are fairly difficult to access. You aren't likely to find many other agate hunters at this site. There are lots of visitors here, but very few of them leave the parking area.

Starting from Cape Arago you can drop down two trails; one that goes north giving you access to North Cove, and another trail goes south and drops down to South Cove.

The gravels here are exceptional. One of the largest agates I've ever seen was found in this area. Remember that big agates are usually hidden amongst larger rocks and gravel, and there is no shortage of bigger materials here to explore!

This site once again deserves a special safety warning. Very jagged, rocky shorelines combined with big waves and narrow beaches means that you should be very alert. Let common sense prevail. Some areas here should clearly be avoided, especially on days when the ocean is rough. Never put yourself in a dangerous situation just so you can collect pretty rocks.

Other Attractions:

Cape Arago is the attraction here! This is one of my favorite sites on the coast and the views are absolutely spectacular. Even if you don't scramble down to the beach, watching the monster waves crash into towering basalt cliffs is as good here as anywhere on the Oregon Coast.

This is a great site to watch for a variety of ocean critters. There are excellent tidepools with starfish, anemones, etc. Harbor seals and sea lions are abundant on rocky islands. Surfers report that sharks are commonly sighted in this area. Bring a pair of binoculars, and note that this is a marine protected area.

29. Seven Devils (Merchant Beach)

Directions:

From Bandon, go north about 4.5 miles and turn left on Seven Devils Road. Continue north for about 5 miles to arrive at the Seven Devils State Recreation Site.

It's worth noting that you can also access this beach from Charleston, but the Seven Devils Road turns to a dirt road just north of here. Easiest access is from the south side mentioned above.

Beachcombing:

This is an excellent site with access to several miles of fairly isolated agate producing beaches. There are limited public accesses here so a person willing to do some hiking can get to some spots that don't get visited all that often.

The parking area is at Merchant Beach. There is a restroom and a small picnic area. Walk north about 1.5 miles and you will reach Agate Beach (a name like that is always a good sign). Another mile north is Sacchi Beach.

Several creeks drain onto the beaches in this area that can carry some fresh gravel. I have found this site to be hit-or-miss just like many other beaches in Oregon. Many days it will be predominantly sandy and poor hunting, but time is right and there can be some good pickin' here.

On my last visit to this site I didn't do all that well on agates, but there were some excellent driftwood piles and I found some great pieces to bring home.

Other Attractions:

Not many people know that there was actually a short-lived gold rush on the southern Oregon Coast, and this was near one of the richest areas. You can actually use a gold pan and recover tiny specks of gold dust among the sands here! If you want to have a uniquely Oregon experience, bring along a gold pan and see if you can find some of this beach gold.

One of the richest mining sites was at Whiskey Run Beach, which is about 1.5 miles to the south. Go south about a mile on Seven Devils Road and turn off on Whiskey Run Lane for an access to the beach right where the gold rush occurred.

There is gold present throughout the sands from the mouth of the Coquille River up to the Seven Devils Rec Site. The trick is to find concentrations of black sand, which are composed of iron minerals that are much heavier than the normal blonde sands. The mouth of Whiskey Run Creek is a popular spot for local gold prospectors.

30. Bullards Beach

Directions:

Heading north on Highway 101 from Bandon, look for the turnoff just after you go across the Coquille River bridge. Take the Bullards Beach Road and follow the signs for access to the beach and lighthouse.

This is a larger-than-average state park with abundant camping sites for tents and RVs. There are equestrian trails, horseshoe pits, good picnicking and other activities.

Beachcombing:

Bullards Beach is one of the more popular agate hunting spots in Oregon. Access is easy and the beach can often be very productive with lots of good gravel that may be present throughout the year.

Of course, when I say "popular," that also means that Bullards is certainly no secret. The last time I visited Bullards was just after a big winter storm, and there were some excellent gravel beds. The agate hunters were out in full force. After 30 minutes of poking around on the beach, I looked around to notice that there were probably 15-20 people within a stone's throw of me doing the same thing. No matter, there were loads of agates and jaspers to be found, and even with that much pressure I was still finding some good material.

Keep in mind, there are good accesses between the main parking lot at Bullards and the Coquille River lighthouse. The road to the lighthouse parallels the ocean just out of sight for about a mile and a half. You can easily pull over and walk right over the sand dune and access the beach with very little effort. A good option if you want to avoid the crowds at the main parking areas.

Other Attractions:

While you are at Bullards Beach you have to go see the Coquille River Lighthouse. It was recently restored after many years of neglect. Tours are available during the summer season.

Bullards Beach is a well-known agate hunting location.

31. Bandon South Jetty Park

Directions:

From downtown Bandon, turn north off Highway 101 and go one block to 1st St SE. Continue west and turn right on Jetty Rd. SW, following along the Coquille River until you reach South Jetty County Park.

Beachcombing:

This is a great access right in Bandon. There can be good gravel here, but it's also very popular so you can expect lots of competition. Just like Bullard Beach to the north, this site can be exceptional pickin', with abundant agates and jaspers. The occasional petrified wood specimen is not unheard of. Plan on timing your visit for the best odds of finding good material here.

The park is located at the south side of the Coquille River. You can park here and walk on the beach for many miles to the south.

There are additional accesses south of here by going south on Beach Loop Road, which follows along the coastline through Bandon for several miles that will get you closer to popular sites such as Coquille Point, Face Rock and

Devil's Kitchen.

Several small creeks enter the beach in this area such as Tupper Creek, Johnson Creek, Crooked Creek and China Creek. Depending on the day you visit you might find better gravels at various spots along Beach Loop Road. Explore!

Other Attractions:

Bandon is a quaint little coastal town. I like it's size; big enough that there are plenty of things to do, yet small enough that it doesn't get quite as hectic during peak tourist season. Explore the downtown for a variety of art galleries, restaurants, bars and breweries. A couple bucks will get you into the Bandon Historical Society Museum where you can learn more about Bandon's claim to fame... cranberries!

32. Cape Blanco

Directions:

From Port Orford, head north on Highway 101 for approximately 4 miles and turn west on Cape Blanco Road. Go another 4 miles to get to the access at the Historic Hughes House (at Sixes River), and an additional mile to get to the Cape Blanco Lighthouse and access at Cape Blanco State Park.

Beachcombing:

This is one of my favorite sites with miles and miles of remote river and beach access. Since Cape Blanco is quite a ways from the major touristy towns, these beaches get a lot less pressure than many others mentioned in this book.

There are excellent gravel bars to explore here. Time it right and this can be one of the best sites on the Oregon Coast. If you are willing to put some miles on your boots, you will be rewarded with some premium agates.

There are several ways to access good hunting areas here. The first is to go to Hughes House which sits above the Sixes River. You can park here and (assuming water levels are low enough) walk right down the river's edge all the way to the ocean. If the water levels are too high, you can still park here and hike a trail for roughly 1/2 mile to access the beach just south of the mouth of Sixes River.

Beaches can also be accessed from the lighthouse. Park at the big parking area just before you get to the lighthouse (in the off-season, the road will be gated and this will be the end of the road.) There are trails here that you can access beaches from both north and south of Cape Blanco. Be aware that you are starting from a higher elevation and these trails aren't heavily used.

An ambitious agate hunter could do a good hike starting at Hughes House, going down the Sixes River to the beach, then south to the lighthouse. This would give you several miles of prime pickin'.

If you want a much easier access here, turn south before the lighthouse and head toward the campground. Go right through the campground (enter the 1-way loop and look for a sign for beach access.) Note that this is a very steep, narrow road down to the beach. No RVs or trailers.

Other Attractions:

If you visit during the summer, take a tour of the Historic Hughes House, an 11-room Victorian-style home built in 1898. The Hughes family raised dairy cattle here and became quite prosperous, eventually acquiring over 1,000 acres around Cape Blanco. The property now makes up a large part of Cape Blanco State Park.

33. Paradise Point

Directions:

Turn west on Paradise Point Road just as you are entering the city limits on the north end of Port Orford. There was an odd lack of signage to indicate there was beach access here, but keep driving west and the road will end at the beach.

Beachcombing:

Paradise Point is one of only two areas (Tseriadun State Recreation Area is about a mile south) that will get you access to the beaches between Port Orford and Elk River. From here, you can walk several miles of beach that are not heavily hunted.

The agate hunting around Port Orford can be exceptional. Find good gravel and you are sure to fill your pockets with some awesome treasures. It is also worth noting that some of the largest agates that I have ever seen came from this general area. If you have been looking for a real "trophy" agate for your collection, a visit to Port Orford might be in order.

Other Attractions:

This is a much sleepier town than many others along the coast, something that I find appealing. If you are a history buff like I am, consider a visit to the Lifeboat Station Museum. Learn about the history of lifeboat operators who risked life and limb to respond to ships in distress. The museum is perched on the cliffs above Nellies Cove.

34. Battle Rock City Park

Directions:

Hard to miss this one. Look for the parking lot right off the Highway on the south end of Port Orford. There is a restroom and Information Center.

Beachcombing:

Port Orford is known for its excellent agate hunting, and this is probably the most obvious and easily accessible beach site. From here you will be able to walk south for several miles.

On my last visit in December, I intended to walk down the shoreline to where Hubbard Creek drains into the Pacific Ocean (about 1 mile). I didn't make it that far, as the gravel was so good that I was moving at a snail's pace the whole time. Lots of nice jellybean-sized agates in a variety of colors from clear to yellow with nice banding. Like many of the beaches around Port Orford, there seems to be less hunting pressure which helps increase your odds of success.

Other Attractions:

Battle Rock gets its name from a little skirmish that happened in 1851 between the early Native Americans and Captain William Tichenor and his men. They arrived to establish the first white settlement (without any agreement from local tribes) and were met with hostility. Nine men used Battle Rock as protection from a large group of the Qua-to-mah tribe. While you are here doing some agate hunting you'll have a chance to read up on the early history of this site.

35. Rocky Point

Directions:

This access is very easy to miss if you aren't paying close attention. Driving south from Port Orford, you will go about 3 miles. Just as the highway starts forming a 2nd passing lane, there is an unmarked road that drops down to the beach. This is a smaller parking area that can only adequately accomodate a few vehicles.

Beachcombing:

This is a good access point to hit lots of nice rocky shoreline south of Port Orford. A short walk north is Rocky Point, and if you were feeling ambitious you could continue walking all the way to Port Orford.

About 2 miles south of this access, the highway turns away from the ocean and access is more difficult. The entire section from Port Orford to where the highway leaves the ocean can be exceptional agate hunting. There are a few turnouts along the highway but they require a pretty treacherous scramble down to the beach. As a result, there is a good 5 mile section here that doesn't get hit very hard by beachcombers. This access is one of the only spots where you can get a vehicle right down to the beach.

Other Attractions:

There are lots of great hikes on the Oregon Coast. One of my favorites is the Humbug Mountain trail. It is a 5.3 mile loop that starts along Highway 101 and climbs to the summit of Humbug Mountain. The first mile is pretty steep but it levels out a bit after that. If you are up for the challenge you will be rewarded with a quiet hike that's generally not too crowded and some exceptional views of the Pacific Ocean.

36. Ophir Beach

Directions:

The access to the beach is south of the "town" of Ophir, about 1.2 miles past the bridge that crosses over Euchre Creek. There is a big, wide turnout and access is easy. Wide open beaches and easy hunting for miles and miles.

Beachcombing:

The few times I have been here there were almost no people, which is always a plus for me. On my last visit, there was a gold prospector here panning gold out of the beach sand. He showed me a little vial full of super-tiny specks of shiny gold dust that he had recovered. Pretty cool!

I haven't found all that many agates at this site, but I know it has good potential. I have found some really awesome jaspers that were very large and turned out great after I put them in the rock tumbler.

I always find larger material here. Big, cobble and tumbled stones in the 4" to 10" size range with a wide variety of colors. I haven't found any "trophy" agates at this site yet, but I know it's just a matter of time. Anywhere that has larger rocks like this definitely has potential to produce big agates. I always find nice smooth stones for the rock garden.

Other Attractions:

If you're looking for a way to entertain the kids then be sure to check out Prehistoric Gardens, a famous roadside attractions that has been around since 1955. Take a self-guided tour through the coastal forest and see 23 life-size replicas of dinosaurs and prehistoric creatures. You won't have a hard time finding it... about 4 miles north of Ophir, there is a big t-rex sculpture right along the highway.

37. Otter Point Park

Directions:

Driving south as you enter Wedderburn, take the exit off Highway 101. You will immediately turn back to the north on the Old Coast Highway. There are several accesses to the beach here. A couple spots are immediately to the left in less than 1/4 mile (across from Knox Lane). If you continue north for about a mile, you will reach the Otter Point Park Beach Access.

Beachcombing:

This site always produces some very interesting materials. This beach is just north of the mouth of the Rogue River, the largest river system in the South Coast Range. There is always lots of larger cobble material here.

Every time I visit this site you could fill buckets with big chunks of white quartz and green jasper material. The jaspers take a nice polish and are commonly fist-sized and larger. This is a fun spot to hunt; there's just so much variety beyond those small black and grey basalt rocks that usually dominate the Oregon Coast.

If you don't have any luck at Otter Point, you can go south on the Old Coast Highway. Go south of the exit and the road will change names to Wedderburn Loop. It will take you to an access point on the North Jetty on the Rogue River.

Other Attractions:

This site is just north of the town of Gold Beach, so there are plenty of places to explore. Take a beautiful drive up the Rogue River toward Agness. If you're really feeling adventurous, there are jet boat tours based out of Gold Beach that can take you 100+ miles up from the mouth of the Rogue River into some of Oregon's wildest country.

38. Gold Beach

Directions:

There is some prime agate pickin' right in the town of Gold Beach. On the north end of town, turn on Harbor Way, then again on South Jetty Rd. You can get to the beach at the South Jetty, and you can follow Oceanside Road for numerous easy accesses to the beach. Basically anywhere in Gold Beach is worth exploring.

My favorite access is called Kissing Rock, about 2 miles south of Gold Beach. There is a large pullout next to a tall rock outcrop with a short trail down to the beach. There will be fewer people here than right in Gold Beach, and it's located at the mouth of Hunter Creek.

Beachcombing:

There is excellent agate hunting at this site. As with several other beaches along the southern Oregon Coast, there is larger gravel here than a lot of other areas. As a result, when you do find an agate you can expect it to be larger than average.

There is a lot of fun variety here too. I always find some agates here, but I also find white, yellow, green and red stones. This is a great site for brecciated jasper that has neat veins shooting through the stones.

My last visit here was in the winter after a large storm. Even though there were plenty of folks out beachcombing, it was still super easy to find agates. I also found one of my all-time favorite pieces of petrified wood at this site.

Gold Beach also attracts tourists during the winter months by hiding glass art floats on the beaches. Keep an eye out for them between February and April. They are hidden between the Rogue River jetty down to Kissing Rock. Look for them hidden above the high tide amongst the grass and driftwood.

Kissing Rock is about 2 miles south of the town of Gold Beach. I visited this site in February and was greeted with gravel beds for as far as I could see.

Other Attractions:

Gold Beach gets its name from miners who discovered gold amongst the sands at the mouth of the Rogue River. The first discovery was made in 1852, not long after the gold rush to California started. Miners sluiced on the beaches at Gold Beach and recovered considerable gold before the deposits were depleted. You can visit the Curry Historical Museum to learn about this interesting part of Oregon's past. Even though most of that gold is long gone, you can still use a gold pan to find tiny specks of gold that were left behind.

39. Pistol River

Directions:

There are good beaches to explore immediately north and south of the mouth of Pistol River, but my favorite access is on the south side. To get there, travel south from Gold Beach for approximately 10 miles. There is a turnout immediately after the bridge over the Pistol River.

Beachcombing:

Lots of excellent beaches to explore at the Pistol River State Scenic Viewpoint. You can hunt the beach and you can search along the banks of the river. Both can be productive depending on the time of year.

This is a great site for jaspers. Usually they are bluish and green colors, but nice deep red jaspers also turn up occasionally. There are big cobbles here so you can expect to find larger treasures. I found a nice big chunk of red jasper that was probably 30 pounds. I left it on the beach for the next person to enjoy. Maybe it's still there?

A quick note to mention is that there was broken vehicle glass in the parking area on my last visit. Unfortunately it is not an uncommon sight these days, particularly at more obscure parking spots along the coast. Make sure you secure your valuables out of sight. I always clean out my glove box and leave it wide open as a way of saying "nothing to steal here, folks!"

Other Attractions:

Windsurfing is so good here that it has been the location of several national championships. The Pistol River Wave Bash occurs every year in early summer. You can come and watch some of the best windsurfers from all around the world compete.

40. McVay Rock

Directions:

This site is about 3.5 miles south of Brookings. From the bridge over the Chetco River, continue south on Highway 101 for about 1.5 miles. Turn right on Pedrioli Drive, continue to Oceanview Drive. Turn south and go another mile to arrive at McVay Rock State Recreation Site. The turnoff can be easy to miss if you are approaching from the north. Look for Seagull Lane.

Beachcombing:

The Chetco River provides abundant gravel along the beaches around Brookings. This site is always productive. I was literally picking up agates within seconds of walking onto the beach on my last visit.

I find smaller sized gravel here than I do up around Gold Beach and Ophir. Most material runs marble-sized and smaller. Hunting here is always good though. Lots of agates, but also colorful rocks with neat variations. Plenty of brecciated jaspers and I always seem to find at least 1 or 2 pieces of sea glass here.

This access is popular because it's close to Brookings. There is a designated dog-exercise area here and most folks here don't even go down to the beach.

Anywhere within a couple miles of Brookings is going to be prime agate hunting. There's good beachcombing all the way down to the California border. This is a great area to explore and try to find those small secluded beaches tucked between the jagged rock outcrops.

Other Attractions:

Brookings is one of the larger towns on the coast, so there are all sorts of activities that you can check out all throughout the year. Art walks, music festivals, chocolate festivals, pirate festivals... if you are there on a weekend then there is likely to be something fun going on.

Made in the USA
Las Vegas, NV
18 November 2021